Be A
Pet Expert

BE A CAT EXPERT

By Gemma Barder

CRABTREE
PUBLISHING COMPANY
WWW.CRABTREEBOOKS.COM

BE A CAT EXPERT

Cats are one of the world's best-loved pets, but how much do you know about these fabulous **felines**? This book is crammed with everything you need to know to become a pet expert, from rare breeds to famous felines and everything in between. Plus there are top tips on how to look after your kitten and help it grow up happy and healthy.

CRABTREE
PUBLISHING COMPANY
WWW.CRABTREEBOOKS.COM

Published in Canada
Crabtree Publishing
616 Welland Avenue
St. Catharines, ON
L2M 5V6

Published in the United States
Crabtree Publishing
347 Fifth Ave,
Suite 1402-145
New York, NY 10016

First published in 2019 by Wayland
Copyright © Hodder and Stoughton, 2019

Author: Gemma Barder

Editorial director: Kathy Middleton

Editors: Dynamo Limited, Robin Johnson

Cover and interior design: Dynamo Limited

Proofreader: Melissa Boyce

Production coordinator
& Prepress technician: Samara Parent

Print coordinator: Katherine Berti

Printed in Canada/122021/CPC20211215

Photographs
(l - left, br - bottom right, c - center, tr - top right)

All images courtesy of Getty Images iStock except:
Cat'chy Images/Shutterstock: front cover and title page l;
Vivienstock/Shutterstock: 7tr; Everett Collection/Alamy: 21br
Pictorial Press Ltd/Alamy: 21c; Tierfotoagentur/Alamy: 23tr

Every attempt has been made to clear copyright. Should there be any inadvertent omission, please apply to the publisher for rectification.

Library and Archives Canada Cataloguing in Publication

Title: Be a cat expert / by Gemma Barder.
Other titles: Cats
Names: Barder, Gemma, author.
Description: Series statement: Be a pet expert |
  Previously published under title: Cats. | Includes index.
Identifiers: Canadiana (print) 20200222120 |
  Canadiana (ebook) 20200222198 |
  ISBN 9780778780151 (hardcover) |
  ISBN 9780778780434 (softcover) |
  ISBN 9781427125576 (HTML)
Subjects: LCSH: Cats—Juvenile literature. | LCSH: Cat breeds—
  Juvenile literature.
Classification: LCC SF445.7 .B37 2021 | DDC j636.8/0887—dc23

Library of Congress Cataloging-in-Publication Data

Names: Barder, Gemma, author.
Title: Be a cat expert / by Gemma Barder.
Description: New York : Crabtree Publishing Company, 2021. |
  Series: Be a pet expert | Includes index.
Identifiers: LCCN 2020015998 (print) | LCCN 2020015999 (ebook) |
  ISBN 9780778780151 (hardcover) |
  ISBN 9780778780434 (paperback) |
  ISBN 9781427125576 (ebook)
Subjects: LCSH: Cats--Juvenile literature.
Classification: LCC SF445.7 .B365 2021 (print) | LCC SF445.7 (ebook) |
  DDC 636.8--dc23
LC record available at https://lccn.loc.gov/2020015998
LC ebook record available at https://lccn.loc.gov/2020015999

CONTENTS

4   ALL KINDS OF CATS
Find out more about the most popular
kitties on the planet.

6   UNFAMILIAR FELINES
Have you ever heard of the Kurilian Bobtail or the Peterbald?

8   CAT CHAT
Understand your cat from head to tail.

10   KITTENS
Learn how to prepare for these adorable bundles of fun.

12   KITTY CARE
Keep your cat healthy and happy with these top tips.

14   THE RIGHT STUFF
Read the dos and don'ts of cat care.

16   CAT COMFORT
Make the perfect home for your pet.

18   POUNCE THROUGH THE PAST
Travel through time with this fascinating guide.

20   FAMOUS FELINES
Everyone's heard of Hello Kitty, but do you know about Unsinkable Sam?

22   CLAWSOME CATS
Meet the loudest, largest, and fluffiest kitties of them all.

24   FIVE FACTS
How many of these crazy cat facts do you know?

26   THE COOLEST CAT
Which breed of cat is best for you?

28   QUIZ!
Are you a pet expert?

31   GLOSSARY

32   INDEX

UNFAMILIAR
FELINES

KITTENS

ALL KINDS OF CATS

Did you know there are 58 recognized **breeds** of **domestic** cats in the world? It's time to get to know some of the most popular ones!

DOMESTIC SHORTHAIR

The world's most popular cat is a mix of different breeds. It's sometimes called a house cat. It has short hair and can be a variety of colors.

FACT FILE

It's official: owning a cat is good for your health!

■ Petting a cat reduces stress levels, which keeps your heart healthy.

■ In a survey, 41 percent of cat owners said they slept better with a cat in their bedroom.

■ Having a pet you love releases a chemical in your brain called oxytocin. This clever chemical not only makes you feel happy, it can also be good for your digestion.

House cats can be many different colors, such as black and white with yellow eyes!

DID YOU KNOW?
There are 80 million domestic shorthair cats in the United States.

BRITISH SHORTHAIR

This cat is the **purebred** version of a domestic shorthair. It has orange-yellow eyes and a thick, short **coat**, which is usually a blue-gray color. British Shorthairs are good-natured, easy to **groom**, and don't have many health problems, which makes them the perfect pets!

MAINE COON

The Maine Coon is one of the largest domestic cats. It can grow to around 3 feet (1 m) long and weighs between 7 and 11 pounds (3–5 kg). It has a long, fluffy coat and a big, bushy tail. The Maine Coon was once used as a farm cat because of its fantastic ability to hunt mice. Now it is a very popular (and very stylish!) pet.

DID YOU KNOW?
A Maine Coon cat had a starring role in the Harry Potter movies! She played caretaker Argus Filch's cat, Mrs. Norris.

PERSIAN

With its short, compact face and little nose, the Persian cat is very easy to recognize. Its coat must be brushed every day so it needs a bit more care than a shorthair, but it is very affectionate and loves to be petted.

This gorgeous kitty needs plenty of pampering and attention, but she deserves it!

UNFAMILIAR FELINES

From **sacred** kitties to cats with no fur, read all about these lesser-known breeds.

This strong and sturdy cat is actually a big softy.

PETERBALD

As the name suggests, these kitties are completely furless, although they are sometimes born with small, soft hairs that disappear as the cats grow. Despite looking a little different than other cats, Peterbalds are very loving and affectionate.

KURILIAN BOBTAIL

Kurilian Bobtails are stocky, clever cats with short, fluffy tails. In their native Kuril Islands (near Japan and Russia) these cats are known as great hunters, but they are very gentle with their owners.

EGYPTIAN MAU

These royal-looking cats are one of the only spotted domestic cat breeds in the world. They are also super speedy! They were worshiped in ancient Egypt as sacred animals. Today, pictures of these cats can be found on statues and carvings and inside Egyptian tombs.

FACT FILE

Some of the most recognizable big cats are also some of the most **endangered**.

■ Tigers: The Malayan tiger is the most endangered tiger on the planet. Scientists believe there are only 250 to 340 of these tigers left in the world. Their biggest threats are the loss of their natural habitats in Malaysia and **poaching**.

■ Lions: Although not as endangered as some tigers, African lion **populations** are decreasing. There are about 20,000 lions left in the wild.

48 mph

30 mph

An Egyptian mau can run up to 48 miles per hour (77 kph), while many other domestic cats can run only around 30 miles per hour (48 kph).

CAT CHAT

Do you know what it means when your cat **purrs** or what your cat's tail is trying to tell you? It's time to find out if you are right!

TAIL

A cat uses its tail mainly for balance, but the tail also gives clues about your cat's mood. A tail in the air with the tip pointed toward you is a friendly greeting. A swaying, halfway-down tail means your cat is confused or trying to make a decision.

FACT FILE

Cats rub the sides of their heads and bodies against people and objects for several reasons:

- to say hello

- to spread their scents and mark their territories

- to pick up scent information from cats or other animals

EARS

A cat can move its ears a lot, and their ears can tell you a lot about how your cat is feeling. Soft or rounded ears mean your cat is relaxed. Ears pointing straight up mean your cat is alert, and ears flat back or to the side mean your cat is **anxious** or frightened.

TUMMY

When a cat rolls over and shows you its tummy, the cat is saying hello and showing you it is happy. Unlike dogs, however, cats don't usually want their tummies rubbed. Most would prefer a quick nose scratch instead!

DID YOU KNOW?

Cats purr when they are happy, and they can also purr to keep themselves calm. They often purr when you take them to the **vet**, or even before they have kittens!

EYES

If a cat slowly blinks its eyes at you, that's a good sign. The slow blink means the cat trusts you and isn't afraid. When you meet a new cat, try blinking slowly to show the cat you are just as relaxed.

KITTENS

There's no doubt that kittens are some of the cutest baby animals around, but they also need a lot of special care and attention.

CHOOSING YOUR KITTEN

Make sure you pick the right kitten before you bring it into your home. Remember that longhair breeds need plenty of grooming. Talk to the owners of the kitten and ask to meet its parents, too, to see what sort of cat it might grow into.

DID YOU KNOW?

Kittens can sleep up to 18 hours a day!

BRINGING IT HOME

Your kitten will find its new home a little strange at first, so you will need to be very calm and patient when it first arrives. Put its bed in a quiet, cozy spot and let your kitten explore at its own pace.

ON THE MENU

Your kitten may not eat much when you first bring it home, but soon it will be gobbling up whatever you put out for it. Kittens can eat wet or dry food, but try to buy special kitten food that contains many of the vitamins they need.

FACT FILE

■ Kittens are born in groups called litters. There are between one and nine kittens in a litter.

■ They can't see clearly or hear very well until they are three weeks old.

■ Kittens become fully grown when they are between six months and a year old.

■ The word "kitten" means "little cat" in old French.

KITTY CARE

From feeding to grooming, learn everything you need to know to keep your cat happy.

PURR-FECT GROOMING

Cats do a great job of keeping themselves clean. However, there are still plenty of things for you to do. Brush your cat at least once a week to get rid of any dead skin and tangled fur, and check your cat's eyes and ears to make sure they are clean and healthy.

FOOD AND DRINK

Like most animals, cats need a supply of fresh, clean water to drink at all times (especially in warm weather). Choose a cat food that contains taurine (a type of amino acid) because it is great for their hearts and eyes.

KITTY LITTER

When cats are indoors they like to use **litter boxes** as toilets. Make sure you keep the litter box in the same spot so your cat knows where to find it. Clean out any soiled litter as soon as you spot it. Cats can be quite fussy and your cat might not use a dirty litter box!

PAW PATROL

Cats love exploring, so from time to time they may get things like pebbles, dirt, or even small toys stuck in their paws. Keep an eye on how your cat is walking and check its paws regularly.

DID YOU KNOW?

People often think cats love to drink cream and milk, but many cats can't **digest** dairy.

DANGEROUS PLANTS

Although most cats are picky about their food, you may need to be careful about some plants that come into your home. Lilies are particularly poisonous to cats, and their pollen can be accidentally knocked into food. If you have a cat that likes to nibble on grass, try growing cat-friendly plants such as catnip and mint.

FLEA AND WORM TREATMENT

Your cat can pick up fleas and worms easily, especially if it is an outdoor cat. An adult cat should have a flea and worm treatment every three months. Treatments can be as simple as placing a cream on your cat's back or mixing in some medicine with its food.

MICROCHIPPING

Microchipping is a simple, painless procedure in which a vet places a tiny microchip (about the size of a grain of rice) under your cat's skin. If your cat ever gets lost, the microchip can be scanned to find out where the cat lives.

Spend quality time with your cat by playing with balls, toy mice, and pieces of ribbon and string.

FACT FILE
BATH TIME

Most cats hate to get wet, but if your cat *really* needs a bath:

- ■ Choose a time when your cat is relaxed.
- ■ Place a rubber bath mat on the bottom of the bathtub to keep your cat from slipping.
- ■ Use pet shampoo to avoid drying out your cat's skin.
- ■ Place a small cotton ball in each of your cat's ears.
- ■ After the bath, wrap your cat in a large, warm towel.

THE RIGHT STUFF

Here are some top tips for looking after your cat. Make sure you have everything covered before bringing home your fluffy bundle.

DO:

Check if any family members are allergic to cats before you bring your pet home. ✔

Keep any top-floor windows closed and locked to prevent curious kitties from climbing out. ✔

Play with cat toys! Cats love to chase and pounce, so get your kitty a little toy mouse or feathers on a string. ✔

Give your cat space when it is eating in case you make it nervous. ✔

OUTDOORS OR INDOORS?

Some cat breeds need to be kept indoors, while others are happier if they can wander outdoors wherever they want. Ask your vet if you aren't sure where to keep your cat.

DON'T:

Don't feed your cat too much. Overweight kittens can develop health diseases and other problems.

Don't pet their tails. Cats love to have their backs, ears, and chins scratched, but they don't like people touching their tails.

Don't be negative. Cats don't respond well to shouting and may become afraid of you.

Don't skip flea treatments. They are easy to do and will keep your cat from feeling itchy.

✔ FOOD FOR CATS ✖

 cat food

 green beans

 garlic

 raisins

 cooked lamb

 hard-boiled eggs

 grapes

 raw fish

 cooked, skinless chicken

 peas

 onions

 seeds

CAT COMFORT

Learn how to give your cat the best home and show it just how much you care.

A bed with a cover can give a new cat somewhere to snuggle up and feel safe!

HOME SWEET HOME

No matter how far your cat roams during the day, it will always need a safe, cozy spot to come home to. Give your cat its own bed with a soft, warm cushion to snuggle up on. Wash the bedding at least once a week.

SLOW AND STEADY

Take things slowly when you move into a new house or bring home a new cat. Introduce your cat to one room at a time and let it decide where to explore next. Cats can be nervous in new surroundings, so give them time to get used to their new home.

SCRATCHING IS GOOD!

Cats need to scratch. It helps them file down their claws and keep them healthy. A scratching post can be a great way to prevent claw marks on your furniture.

DID YOU KNOW?

Cats can sleep up to 17 hours a day. They are crepuscular, which means they are most active at dawn and dusk.

FACT FILE

Why do cats scratch? You might get annoyed at your kitty for scratching your bedposts or the corner of your favorite chair, but scratching is very important for your cat. Here's why:

- It keeps their claws healthy.
- It marks their territory.
- It spreads their scent.
- It helps them stretch.

POUNCE THROUGH THE PAST

Cats have been worshiped, given royal protection, and become Internet stars. Find out about their incredible history!

CHINA

About 2,500 years ago, the ancient Egyptians gave a cat to the emperor of China. Later, Egyptian cats were bred with Chinese wildcats, which resulted in new breeds such as Siamese and Burmese cats.

2000 B.C.E.　　　　**500 B.C.E.**　　　　**900s C.E.**

EGYPT

The first record of cats living with humans can be found almost 4,000 years ago in ancient Egypt. People kept cats to stop mice and rats from destroying crops. The cats were so good at their jobs that people could grow plenty of food.

WALES

Cats became known for their **vermin**-busting skills. In the tenth century, the king of Wales gave cats official royal protection. That meant anyone who killed a cat could be sentenced to death!

DID YOU KNOW?

Cats became sacred creatures in ancient Egypt and were often associated with the goddess Bastet.

2 million

25 billion

There are more than 2 million cat videos on YouTube, and they have been watched 25 billion times!

ROYAL REUNION

When Queen Victoria (1819–1901) added a cat to her household, cats became very fashionable and popular as family pets.

1300s C.E.

1800s

1990s

WITCHCRAFT

In the Middle Ages, cats became associated with witches and witchcraft, and by the middle of the fourteenth century they had become less popular. With fewer cats, **rodent** populations grew and rodent-infested homes, towns, and cities were much more common.

POPULAR PET

In the 1990s, cats officially took over from dogs as the world's most popular pet! Their popularity can be seen everywhere, from books and movies to the Internet, where you can watch millions of videos of people's beloved cats.

FAMOUS FELINES

Have you ever heard of the unsinkable cat? Or the kitty that's met some of the most important people in the world? Keep reading to discover more.

HELLO KITTY

Hello Kitty was created in 1974 to appear on a change purse. Today she is featured on everything from books and bandages to clothes and accessories. Hello Kitty is named after Alice's cat in the Lewis Carroll book *Through the Looking-Glass*. Although her creators are Japanese, Hello Kitty herself lives in London, England!

FACT FILE

Things you might not know about Hello Kitty:

- She is a Japanese Bobtail.
- Her full name is Kitty White.
- She has a twin sister named Mimmy.
- She is five apples tall and weighs three apples.
- Her birthday is November 1.

CHIEF MOUSER

There have been many "chief **mousers**" at 10 Downing Street, the official residence of the prime minister of the United Kingdom—including Larry. This cat has met some important people, such as former U.S. president Barack Obama, but he can be a little grumpy with other cats.

UNSINKABLE SAM

Sam was a very lucky cat who lived on both German and British ships during World War II (1939–1945). He survived three shipwrecks before being taken back to England to live the rest of his life in a home for sailors.

Sam was rescued from this aircraft carrier after it was torpedoed in 1941.

$50

$1 million

The average cat costs $50. Grumpy Cat was thought to be worth $1,000,000!

GRUMPY CAT

Grumpy Cat became an Internet sensation in 2012 when her owner's brother posted a picture of her online. She soon became a star, with posters, books, and T-shirts showing her adorable face. Grumpy Cat's real name was Tardar Sauce and she had a feline version of **dwarfism**.

CLAWSOME CATS

Who are the oldest, longest, and smallest cats? They're all here in these pages of feline record breakers!

Ligers can be seen only in zoos and nature reserves.

DID YOU KNOW?
The biggest cat in the world is a liger (a cross between a male lion and a female tiger) named Hercules who is 10.9 feet (3.33 m) long!

OLD-TIMER

Creme Puff was a cat born in 1967 in Austin, Texas. She lived for 38 years and three days—double the average life span of a cat. Creme Puff's owner believed the cat's long life was due to the unusual food he fed her, including bacon and broccoli.

ONE LOUD PURR

The loudest purr ever recorded was made by a cat named Merlin from a town in England. He was recorded at 67.8 decibels, which is as loud as a car going 65 miles per hour (105 kph)!

TEENY TINY KITTY

A Himalayan-Persian cat named Tinker Toy was the world's smallest cat. He was only 2.8 inches (7 cm) tall and 7.5 inches (19 cm) long when he was fully grown!

Tinker Toy was a Himalayan-Persian cat, like this one!

BEST BY A WHISKER

Missi, a Maine Coon cat from Finland, officially had the longest whiskers of any domestic cat in the world. Her fabulous feelers measured 7.5 inches (19 cm) long!

BIG AND BEAUTIFUL

Maine Coons really like to show off when it comes to being the biggest and best. In 2010, a Maine Coon in Reno, Nevada, named Stewie was measured at 4 feet (1.23 m) long! He still holds the record for being the longest cat ever.

Maine Coon cats are large, fluffy, and beautiful.

FIVE FACTS

Have you ever wondered why your kitten is so sleepy or who invented the cat flap? Get ready to discover five things you never knew about cats.

1 CATS CAN'T TASTE SWEET THINGS

Because the tiny cells inside a cat's taste buds are formed differently than in other animals, kitties can't taste sugar.

2 A CAT'S NOSE IS UNIQUE

The bumps on a cat's nose are similar to a human fingerprint. No two cats have the same noseprint.

3 NEWTON MADE LIFE EASIER FOR CATS

The famous scientist Sir Isaac Newton invented the cat flap. The story goes that Newton's cat kept opening the door to his laboratory, interfering with his experiments with light. To solve this, he invented a small door that would allow his cat to move between rooms without letting in too much light.

SIR ISAAC NEWTON
(1642–1727)

4 CATS CAN BE RIGHT- OR LEFT-PAWED

Just like humans are right-handed or left-handed, cats like to use either their right or left paws for simple tasks. What's even more interesting is that most male cats are left-pawed and most female cats are right-pawed!

5 KITTENS GROW IN THEIR SLEEP

Kittens produce the special hormone they need to grow only when they are fast asleep, which is why kittens spend most of their time snoozing!

THE COOLEST CAT

Find out what type of cat would be your perfect match.

DO YOU MIND A PET THAT NEEDS A LOT OF CARE?

Maybe

WOULD YOU RATHER HAVE AN INDOOR OR OUTDOOR CAT?

Outdoor

Indoor

No

Playing

WHAT'S BETTER -SNUGGLING OR PLAYING WITH TOYS?

Snuggling

Not really

Yes

DO YOU LOVE CUDDLES?

They're OK

DOES STYLE MATTER TO YOU?

A bit

DO YOU HAVE ANY OTHER PETS?

Yes

No

Um...

IT'S TIME TO BRUSH YOUR CAT. WHO DOES IT?

Me!

Totally

WOULD YOU TELL YOUR CAT ALL YOUR SECRETS?

Possibly

A bit

DO YOU MIND BEING THE CENTER OF ATTENTION?

Not at all

SHORTHAIR
You don't mind if your cat likes to spend some time alone, as long as it wants to cuddle now and then too. You'd be great friends from the moment your kitten peeked out of its carrier.

PERSIAN
You love to cuddle with your cat, which is why a Persian would suit you best. You wouldn't mind brushing or petting your cat for hours as long as it curled up and watched your favorite movie with you.

MAINE COON
You would love the attention your super-stylish cat brings with it. Maine Coons need a bit of extra care, but you wouldn't mind sharing your hair-care tips with your pet pal.

QUIZ!

It's time to test everything you have learned in this book! Are you a pet expert?

1 IN WHAT MOVIE DOES A MAINE COON HAVE A STARRING ROLE AS THE CARETAKER'S CAT?

a) *Nanny McPhee*
b) *Harry Potter and the Sorcerer's Stone*
c) *A Series of Unfortunate Events*

2 WHAT IS THE NAME OF A FURLESS CAT BREED?

a) Peterbald
b) Johnbald
c) Alanbald

3 WHAT SHOULD YOU DO WHEN A CAT ROLLS ON ITS BACK?

a) scratch its tummy
b) ignore it
c) say hello and pet its nose

4 WHAT DOES THE WORD "KITTEN" MEAN IN OLD FRENCH?

a) little cat
b) cute
c) big paws

Turn to the next page to read the answers and discover if you are a pet expert!

5
WHERE SHOULD YOU AVOID PETTING A CAT?

a) tail
b) back
c) ears

6
WHY DO CATS NEED TO SCRATCH?

a) to keep their claws healthy
b) to spread their scents
c) both of the above

7
WHY WERE CATS SO POPULAR IN ANCIENT EGYPT?

a) because they helped build the pyramids
b) because they killed vermin and helped crops grow
c) because they were the rulers' favorite animals

9 WHAT IS HELLO KITTY'S FULL NAME?

a) Kitty Brown
b) Kitty Cat
c) Kitty White

10 WHAT TYPE OF CAT HOLDS THE WORLD RECORD FOR THE LONGEST WHISKERS?

a) Persian
b) British Shorthair
c) Maine Coon

8 HOW MANY RECOGNIZED BREEDS OF DOMESTIC CATS ARE THERE IN THE WORLD?

a) 200
b) 17
c) 58

1b 2a 3c 4a 5a 6c 7b 8c 9c 10c

QUIZ ANSWERS

GLOSSARY

allergic
Describing someone who has a physical reaction (such as sneezing or itchy eyes) to cats or other things

anxious
Worried or nervous

breed
A group of animals that shares the same appearance and characteristics

coat
An animal's fur

digest
To break down food

domestic
Living with humans

dwarfism
A medical condition that causes people or animals to be smaller or shorter than average

endangered
At risk of dying out

feline
A cat or relating to cats

groom
To brush and clean a cat and trim its nails

litter
A group of kittens born at the same time to the same mother

litter box
A container that a cat uses as a toilet when it is indoors

mouser
A cat skilled at catching mice

poaching
Illegally hunting or catching animals

population
The total number of one type of animal living in a certain area

purebred
Having parents and grandparents that are the same breed

purr
The vibrating sound a cat makes

rodent
A rat, mouse, or other small mammal

sacred
Highly valued and important; holy

vermin
Mice and other small animals that cause problems, such as eating crops or damaging property

vet
A medical doctor who treats animals; short for veterinarian

INDEX

A
allergic 14

B
baths 13
beds/bedding 10, 16, 17
breeds 4, 6, 7, 10, 18
British Shorthairs 5

C
cat flaps 25
China 18
coats 5

D
domestic shorthairs 4

E
ears 9, 12, 15
Egypt 7, 18, 19
Egyptian Maus 7
eyes 4, 5, 9, 12

F
fleas 13, 15
food 11, 12, 13, 15, 18, 22
fur 6, 12

G
grooming 5, 10, 12

H
health 4, 5, 15, 16
hunting 5, 6

I
Internet 19, 21

K
kittens 6, 9, 10–11, 24, 25
kitty litter 12
Kurilian Bobtails 6

L
ligers 22
lions 7, 22
litters 6, 11

M
Maine Coons 5, 23
microchipping 13

N
noses 5, 9, 24

P
paws 12, 25
Persians 5, 23
Peterbalds 6
plants 13
purring 8, 9, 22

Q
Queen Victoria 19

R
rubbing 8, 9

S
scratching ... 9, 15, 16, 17
sleeping 10, 17, 24

T
tails 5, 6, 8, 15
tigers 7, 22
toys 12, 13, 14
tummies 9

V
vitamins 11

W
water 12
witches 19
worms 13